*For those brave souls
who represent themselves
in court.*

TABLE OF CONTENTS

Chapter 2 | Take-Off:
Issuing & Defending Claims

Chapter 3 | Keeping the Plane in the Air: Case Management & The Proceedings 151

Chapter 4 | Fully Armed & Loaded: Disclosure, Court Orders & N244s 185

Chapter 5 | The Dogfight: Evidence & Trial

Chapter 6 | The Mindset of a Fighter Pilot: Tactics

Published by Redwood Legal Ltd
138-140 Southwark Street
London SE1 0SW

Warning – Disclaimer
The purpose of this book is to educate and entertain. The author and/or publisher do not guarantee that anyone following these techniques, suggestions, tips, ideas, or strategies will become successful. The author and/or publisher shall have neither liability nor responsibility to anyone with respect to any loss or damage caused, or alleged to be caused, directly or indirectly, by the information contained in this book.

ISBN: 978-1-71696-617-0 (print)

Editor: Kinga Stabryla
Junior Assistant Editor: Klaudia Jędrzejczyk
Cover design: Kinga Stabryla
Cover illustration: Nate Fakes
Book layout and design: Slaven Kovačević
Photographer: Kinga Stabryla

PREFACE

I have chosen to use the analogy of Fighter Pilots in this book. This seems, to me, the perfect metaphor for civil litigation as it helps a litigant in person to get into the right mindset. Whilst a pilot might have a very good aeroplane he might not be a very good pilot. He could, therefore, be defeated by an opponent in an inferior aeroplane with greater experience. In this analogy, of course, the case is the plane and the pilot is the individual running the claim. I have seen many good claims ruined because they were badly run or the individual found themselves up against a rich opponent who could afford clever lawyers. Combat in the skies is not something the Average Joe has any experience of, and the same is true of the complex procedural rules of civil litigation.

Only a fool would play the game without having learned the rules. Whilst you might get away with riding a skateboard, a bicycle or even driving a car without ever having any training, would you get into the cockpit of an aeroplane knowing what you are doing? Have you ever seen the inside of the cockpit of an aeroplane?! I doubt anyone could take off or land a plane properly without knowing what all those buttons on the consoles did.

Moreover, just as in the case of flying there are not only the laws of aerodynamics (the laws of the land), but there are also complex procedural rules with a whole system of air traffic control in place. So, it is that civil litigation has a complex set of rules, called the Civil Litigation Rules, brought in by Lord Woolf, by means of the Access to Justice Act 1999.

Now you could try and go it alone and I am certainly not saying that you have to know these rules in detail (key areas are dealt with in this book), but to get a real jump on your opponent it is worth dipping into them... or at the very least knowing that they are there, all freely available online. I say this because civil proceedings are a dogfight and it is those who play the game well who come away winners. I will cover an example or two of how you can turn these rules to your advantage later in the book.

It is important to understand that where civil litigation is concerned you are engaged in a solo activity in which the best man is likely to win. Sure, it is a big advantage to be in a spitfire rather than an old bi-plane from the first world war, but you are primarily engaged in an entrepreneurial and commercial endeavour – this is not about "justice" or other lofty ideals. It is about winning. Do not get engaged in civil litigation if you are just fighting for your rights or a just cause. That is the province of the rich, celebrities and media types. Even having a strong claim with real merit is not conclusive. It is simply just like having a spitfire. It will certainly make a difference, but it will not get you over the wire. It is a question of who is at the controls and what they do with the aeroplane.

So, do not do what most disgruntled claimants and defendants do. They suffer from the illusion that they can handle it all themselves and the court and the judge is somehow going to be entirely sympathetic and immediately see how badly they have been wronged and give them instant justice. Not true! Courts and judges are extremely busy and fortune favours the prepared. Facing a battle in court – just like life or an aerial dogfight – can be a complicated affair.

Unfortunately in civil litigation, you have to pay quite a lot of money to get a professional to take over the controls and fly the plane for you and in cases allocated to the small claims track you are unlikely to get your legal fees back, even if you win. This is probably why you are reading this book.

So this is your very own, "Paperback Wing Man."

Warning Note!

You need to make sure that any book or legal resource you use online is up to date. The law changes all the time! There were big changes to civil litigation in April 2013 and again in 2018 and since that time there have been many judgments that have updated and clarified those statutory laws. Here is an example of why this caveat could be important:

> **CASE STUDY: PERSONAL INJURY CLAIM**
> Let's say you have a personal injury claim. As things currently stand if it is under £1,000 for the physical damage itself then it will almost certainly be designated as a "small claim". This means you will not be liable to pay the legal costs of your opponent, even if you lose. Nor will they have to pay yours, if you instruct a lawyer. But under the recent Civil Liability Act 2018 this will almost certainly change and by the Spring of 2020 it could go up to £5,000, certainly for road traffic personal injury. So this danger of having to pay legal costs will only occur for a personal injury claim of above £5,000. A pretty significant change. Far more claimants will now run their own personal injury cases without legal help.

Alongside this book, we provide information on our website at www.courtwingman.com and YouTube channel to ensure you are kept up to date as well as provide you with supplementary materials.

Who is this book for?

This is a book for those individuals or small businesses, whether a claimant or a defendant, who have a civil dispute based in the jurisdiction of England & Wales and want to run the case themselves. Such people are called "litigants in person" to distinguish them from those claims where a lawyer has been instructed. There are increasing numbers of litigants in person in the courts these days and it is a growing problem: access to justice has been made more and more difficult by government cuts to the funding of the legal system, whether legal aid cuts or simple cuts to court staff and administration.

Flying the plane on your own may be the only real option if you have decided that it is un-economic to pay a lawyer to run it for you or if you distrust lawyers. But do you go into battle without any help at all?

This book will help you by giving guidance on how to run your claim. It may be a small, fast track or multi-track claim.[1] Cases which are over £25,000 are usually allocated to the multi-track, and those need a word of warning. They are likely to take a 2-day trial or more and involve more complex procedures. Frankly, I would advise you to take legal advice, although nothing is stopping you doing it yourself if you want to... just make sure you follow the rules provided in the Civil Procedure Rules. ("CPR".) I do touch on these claims in the book, and in many ways, they are no different to fast track claims (£10,000-£25,000), so it is relatively easy to cover them. But do please think carefully about obtaining at least a little judicious legal advice from a lawyer on the fast track and nearly mandatorily on the multi-track.

If your claim is a small claim and well under the £10,000 threshold (except for personal injury and housing disrepair[2]) then you need only read those sections that are relevant. The sections on legal costs will be less relevant for you because the normal rule on the small claims track is that the loser does not have to pay the winner's legal costs, which usually keeps lawyers out. But be careful about automatically assuming a low-value claim will always be allocated to the small claims track and that the rule about legal costs will always apply. Take note in particular of the first chapter in part 1 - "Small claims and allocation: a common misconception."

Who is this book not for?

This book is not for people with an employment dispute or a family dispute. Such cases are usually heard in special courts (the Employment Tribunal or Family Courts). Nor is this book for criminal matters.

Whilst it is of general assistance to those with personal injury claims (personal injury claims are civil claims heard in the county courts and

---

1   "Tracks" are what the courts put you on after you have issued a claim and they allocate to one of these three tracks in the vast majority of cases. Read on for an explanation of how these work.
2   Personal injury and housing disrepair claims are exceptions and have a lower threshold. Currently, this is £1,000 for personal injury claims in respect of physical injury, leaving aside any consequential losses of the injury and £1,000 for housing disrepair claims CPR 27.1(2).

so they share the same basic rules), you should be aware that the book does not specifically focus on this sector, which has a whole set of special rules and important changes happening. You are advised to look elsewhere for help with such claims if you need to go beyond the basics. You should also consider using a no win no fee lawyer, of which there are many and so you may well not need a guide book like this altogether.

There is also a whole range of other specialist claims where, frankly, you would be better off finding a lawyer to do it for you, certainly if you are forced to issue proceedings or are defending an issued claim. This could be a dispute of a high value such that it is allocated to the "multi-track" by the courts or it might simply be too complex for the layman. Examples might be intellectual property matters, libel, complex or large scale commercial disputes, contests wills and probate, and cohabitation property disputes (to name just a few).

At this point, I can almost hear you saying, "Surely the court system should be open to everyone?!" Of course, the court system should be open to everyone, however big or complex their case, and there have indeed been notable examples where litigants in person have managed their case. For example, as a young lawyer, I used to go and watch the famous "McLibel" case at the Royal Courts of Justice on The Strand. This was a case that two litigants in person defended themselves against the mighty McDonald's, and it lasted for months, if not years. It was a victory for them in one sense, as McDonald's failed to win on all counts, but they had to give up years of their lives to run it.

Despite this example and quite frankly, I have seen too many people get into hot water where there was high value or complexity involved, such that my general advice is to get a lawyer involved. There are always exceptions, of course, and I should perhaps add that I have on a few occasions had clients who had run their cases themselves initially, even issuing claims, and subsequently asked us to represent them when matters started to become complex. This saved them money because they only turned to the lawyers when necessary.

If your claim is complex, but not sufficiently high value to justify the use of lawyers then you may want to question whether it is wise to bring the claim in the first place. "Pick your battles", as they say.

What is this book's focus?

It is important that this not be an academic book but an entirely practical one and that you get a real sense of what it is like to be fighting the aerial battle in the civil courts. This book draws on real-life examples of cases that I have personally run in the county courts. Occasionally, I refer to these case studies in the book, highlighting them in their separate boxes so you can skip them if they are not relevant to your case. Over time I will be building a library of such cases on the website.

This is not intended to be a dry and technical exposition of the law on the procedure (there are plenty of other books that do this), but a real aid to fighting your case. As well as providing you with tools, a lot of what this book is about is giving you the courage to do it alone. I want you to know by the end of the book what it is like to have been in a dog fight.

It also does not focus on "substantive" law (Ie. the laws of the land). If you want a proper study of the elements of contract law, negligence, or misrepresentation then look elsewhere. There are plenty of solid academic tomes on the English law and you do not need me to add to the pile. This is what law students have to study but it is, in fact, surprisingly redundant when it comes to actual proceedings as disputes rarely centre on issues of law. In the vast majority of cases, the law is pretty clear and the battle is in fact about a whole range of other tactical, evidential, and procedural issues.

I do, however, deal with issues around the substantive law in the section on causes of action. This is because you may have the problem of complexity in your cause of action that prevents you from bringing a claim properly in the first place and so I devote a small section on it. It is important to have first bottomed out which "runway" to the courts it is you are using, as in certain cases without pleading your cause of action carefully you could run into trouble.[3] You do sometimes have to lay out the legal framework.

This book does not take a black and white viewpoint on whether or not to use lawyers to assist you in your case. For instance, you may wish

---

3   If there is serious legal complexity in your cause of action, this is another area where you will want to turn to a lawyer for help.

to use lawyers, on a limited, "advice-only" basis.[4] So this book is also a guide for individuals or businesses who want to have some involvement in their case but not use lawyers outright. The book will help you make the correct decision here.

Using lawyers is not an "either/or" situation, in my view. Many of my most successful cases are with clients to whom I have provided limited legal advice and assistance at key points of the litigation process, without actually going on the court record and formally representing them. Others have run the case themselves and then at a certain point in the litigation decided, perhaps for tactical reasons, to bring in the lawyers wholesale. This can be a smart tactical move, depending on the scale and complexity of the case. Since this book majors on tactics, it would be foolish to exclude one possible tactical move, which is simply to hand the case over to a law firm.

Indeed, if cash is tight, it may be that you need a lawyer who will represent you on a "no win no fee" basis. Even in small claims under £10,000 new "damages-based agreements" can sometimes be used. So, even if you have a small claim you might want to inform yourself about the different types of services lawyers can offer you - it is important tactically that you are aware of how lawyers can help. Using a lawyer judiciously could give you extra re-power in the battle to come.

And be in no doubt, a battle it is. You should be calm, cool and collected about it and present yourself professionally if you want to win.

---

4   Read below for more on this and how a lawyer can help you. The technical term for this type of retainer is "unbundled legal services" but I prefer the term "Lawyer Lite".

Introduction

LIFE IN THE SKIES

THE UK COURT SYSTEM

The introduction describes how the system works, what the rules of the game are and in which arena you are operating. The aerial battle for a fighter pilot takes place in a special, rarified place, high up in the skies and there are different sets of rules – ones governing Civil Litigation. The arena you will be fighting is likewise rarified, and different sorts of rules and laws apply. Having a basic understanding of the legal framework is a must.

The System

This part describes how the system works, what the rules of the game are, and in which arena you are operating. The aerial battle for a fighter pilot takes place in a special, rarified place, high up in the skies and there are different sets of rules – the laws of aerodynamics, for example, or the rules of the Civil Aviation Authority. Civil litigation is no different. The arena you will be fighting is likewise rarified, and different sorts of rules and laws apply. So you need to have a basic understanding of the legal framework.

The arena is, of course, the county courts of England & Wales and the rule book that is used in all civil litigation is, The Civil Procedure Rules (easily accessed online). No normal human being is likely to be able to decipher the Civil Procedure Rules without bleeding from the forehead and people are rightly aggrieved when judges apply it as if a litigant in person is expected to understand it! It is ridiculous. What this means in practice is that judges bend over backward to accommodate litigants in person in court and this can even be an advantage. They also tend to be flexible – where litigants in person are involved (not otherwise). This means you will find that they might not mind if court orders have been breached and the rules were broken. If the other side is represented then their lawyer too is increasingly expected to help a litigant in person.

There is also a White Book, which is an even more detailed book than the Civil Procedure Rules![5] The White Book offers commentary and is meant to explain the Civil Procedure Rules and contains lots of case law on what it all means. Unless you are a barrister this is best avoided. Even solicitors avoid it. Just try and exercise your own common sense when it comes to the Civil Procedure Rules – stand back from the small print and just have a good grasp of the main principles, which I cover later. I personally do not like the Civil Procedure Rules. They just create this huge complexity and any complexity in life then requires professionals to decipher the complexity and so an industry grows up around it and it all means that the Average Joe has to pay a load of money to get access to justice. The game becomes about who has the deepest pockets and who can figure out the technicalities.

Still, there is no point in becoming bitter about it. The Civil Procedure Rules are here to stay and you are going to either need to know them, in so far as it relates to your case, or turn to one of these people who can decipher them for you – lawyers, of course. Rather than get annoyed about it, become good at using it and turn it into an ally rather than see it as an enemy. Like the pilot who actually really gets to grips with all those instrument panels in the cockpit and knows the manual inside out. This is especially important where larger claims are concerned, on the fast and multi-tracks. The court will be less forgiving on these tracks than the small claims track.

---

5   This is a special book for pilots. My father was a pilot and whenever we used to go flying he used to have a big briefcase and he had this book in it. It was white too! It had a lot of technical information in it and he always used to take it on flights in the single-prop piper airplane. He used to fly out of a local farmer's field in the eighties.

Small Claims: A Common Misconception

I need to correct a common misconception at this point. You may have a low-value claim of well under £10,000 and you have been told, after surfing online, that you have a "small claim". This online advice has given you the impression that you do not have to worry about having to pay legal costs because lawyers are kept out of proceedings. You may also have been told the system is much simpler than normal claims and even been given the impression there is a special "small claims court".

But I have had so many experiences where problems arose out of this misconception that I want to clear up the confusion in this area. It will be especially relevant for people who have claims of a higher amount, knocking around the £10,000 mark, and are wondering, "is it a small claim or not?" But even lower value claims could be designated outside the remit of the small claims. If a claim is not allocated to the small claims track you are facing the risk of a large legal bill from an opponent who uses a lawyer. (You may also feel obliged to use lawyers yourself and so generate your own legal bill.) Whilst the vast majority of low-value claims will be allocated to the small claims "track" (not court), it is not automatic and some claims that appear to be appropriate for the small claims track are sometimes allocated to a higher track.

People are wrong to think that there is some sort of a special "small claims court". (I think maybe they confuse it with the American model.) There is not. In fact, any value claim is just a claim when it is first issued, and for some time afterward, until it is officially allocated to a "track". There are three possible tracks that your case will be sent down by the court officials when a claim is first issued. These tracks are (thresholds correct at date of writing):

- ❖ The Small Claims Track (typically claims up to £10,000)
- ❖ The Fast Track (typically £10,000- £25,000)
- ❖ The Multi-Track (over £25,000)

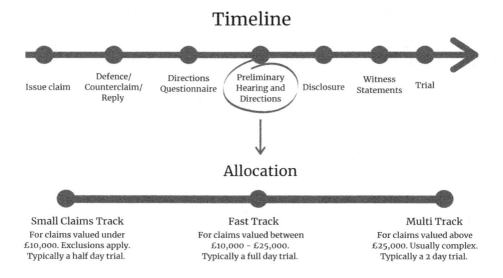

The above timeline graphically illustrates the way in which a claim is just a claim when first issued and is <u>not</u> allocated to a track until some way into the proceedings. Indeed, the Preliminary Hearing & Directions stage could be an allocation hearing. Different rules apply to each track but they are <u>not</u> separate courts. It is the same judges, the same courts, and the same law of both substantive law and the law of procedure that applies. Sure, there are special procedures in respect of small claims, most notably the fact that you do not get your legal costs back if you win. This special procedure overturns a basic principle of civil litigation. This basic principle says that the loser has to pay the winner's costs of the proceedings. This means that, in effect, lawyers are often – *though not always* – kept out of small claims track case, otherwise there are more similarities between the tracks than you might realise. This has important implications.[6]

So, why is it so important for us to correct this common misconception?

---

6   For example, when I represented individuals and small businesses against banks during the financial mis-selling scandals around the time of the 2008 recession, I often found that the banks would instruct high-flying lawyers to fight off consumers, as a policy decision.

(1) DANGER OF STRIKE-OUT

As can be seen, it takes a while for a claim to be allocated to one of these three tracks and you can be quite advanced in terms of the stage of proceedings and the number of legal costs that have been incurred by the time that it is. If you do something wrong in your claim form or your particulars of claim early on (which commonly happens with litigants in person) an opponent can apply to have the claim struck out. A hearing might then be listed for an hour or two at the county court, a special hearing to deal solely with this issue. (Not on the overall merits of your claim, which the court is not at all interested in at that stage.) This is a very important piece of knowledge for the defendants out there and I personally have often used, rather mischievously, failures in improperly brought claims to give a claimant the runaround.

What happens in such applications is that the matter gets listed for a hearing and the litigant in person is thinking, "What's going on?! I wanted this to be a small claim! And now I have to go to court and risk having my whole case struck out and being on the wrong end of a costs order!"

And if the court decides that you have done something wrong and orders you to go away and fix it, you could be in for an unpleasant surprise. Firstly, the judge will order costs against you. If you are facing a barrister these costs could be considerable (I have seen figures of around £1,000 and as high as £2,500.) Secondly, he might make an order that says, "unless the claim is amended and properly particularised by such and such a date the claim stands struck out."

I have seen this happen a lot. It is more common than you realise. When I was suing banks during the payment protection insurance scandal the banks made a point of it and nearly always applied to have claims struck out. They were rich and could afford to send barristers to court just to intimidate consumers. There were lots and lots of strike-out hearings.

So here is a real concern if you are running a case against a well-heeled opponent. I have seen this happen against public bodies (clinical negligence in the case of the NHS), civil prosecutions against the police (classic case of where the cause of action has not been given sufficient attention by a litigant in person), and large construction companies.

The point is that a lot of strike-out applications occur early on when all that has happened is the statements of the case - or "pleadings". All that happened is that each party laid out their case, filed it at court, and served it on the other party, well before the case has **actually been allocated to a track**. Until it is allocated to the small claims track it is not a small claim and the normal costs sanctions can apply. You cannot elect the small claims track.

Apart from their having been an error in the particulars of claim, because it is a complex cause of action, the other area in which problems occur is where litigants in person frequently try to shoe-horn their claim into the small claims track. It might actually be a higher value than £10,000, but they put £9,999 on the claim form without any real rationale as to why this is so. Now if I am the lawyer for the other side I will lick my lips. If they do not apply to amend their claim, after I have written them a nasty letter, I am going to bring a strike-out application against them. They have not correctly "particularised" their losses, having failed to clearly break them down in a detailed and precise way.

In fact, my experience is that not correctly calculating and specifying individual items of loss is by far a bigger problem than getting the law wrong or not properly explaining why someone has been negligent or broken a contract.

> **LADY VS FINANCIAL INSTITUTION**
>
> In one case a lady came to me with a strike-out problem after she had issued her claim in two parts, in respect of two separate loans, against a financial institution. She had thought she could get under the small claims limit by separating the two loans into two separate claims. But the institution just made a strike-out application saying that the dispute was based on the same facts and the claims should have been joined as one, which would have taken it well over the £10,000 mark and put it on the fast track – where she faced a large legal if she lost. Suddenly it looked like a really bad commercial decision by her to take the risk of bringing this litigation in the first place, and she was really worried about the dangers of losing.

(2) UNDER £10,000 IS NOT ALWAYS A SMALL CLAIM

There are certain criteria that the court applies to its decision on allocation. (Just google "CPR – allocation to track" and you will come up with the relevant section, Part 27.) When it comes to allocation it is not an automatic given that a claim of under £10,000[7] is allocated to the small claims track. This is just the "normal" track (the word used in the CPR). So, for example, if there are a lot of witnesses justifying a trial length of more than half a day, if an expert is needed, or if there is some complexity in the law or a combination of all of these factors then there is a good chance that your case will be allocated to a higher track.

The criteria are all laid out in the CPR:

MATTERS RELEVANT TO ALLOCATION TO A TRACK 26.8

(1) When deciding the track for a claim, the matters to which the court shall have regard include –

(a) the nancial value, if any, of the claim;

(b) the nature of the remedy sought;

(c) the likely complexity of the facts, law or evidence;

(d) the number of parties or likely parties;

(e) the value of any counterclaim or other Part 20 claim and the complexity of any matters relating to it;

(f) the amount of oral evidence which may be required;

(g) the importance of the claim to persons who are not parties to the proceedings;

(h) the views expressed by the parties; and

(i) the circumstances of the parties.

(2) It is for the court to assess the financial value of a claim and in doing so it will disregard –

---

7   Personal injury and housing disrepair claims are exceptions and have a lower threshold Currently this is £1,000 for personal injury claims in respect of the physical injury, leaving aside any consequential losses of the injury and £1,000 for housing disrepair claims CPR 27.1(2).).

> (a) *any amount not in dispute;*
> (b) *any claim for interest;*
> (c) *costs; and*
> (d) *any contributory negligence.*

Now, for most of you reading this with a claim value of well under £10,000 you should not worry – you probably have a simple bog-standard claim like a contractual dispute or a simple negligence case. Obviously, if it is a case of a broken television or a car that does not work properly or a wrongly fitted boiler, a judge is going to laugh a lawyer out of court if they apply to strike out and he will probably just amend the claim form of his own volition if a minor error is made.

But you do need to be aware that in larger value or more complex cases and where you are facing a large corporate, a public body, or an opponent with deep pockets, then you need to be careful to get your particulars of claim absolutely right. Once again the truth is that this is an error where, if you have any doubts, you should get legal advice. Just ask a lawyer to quote you for a limited bit of advice in order to cast his eye over your particulars of claim. If you are a defendant ask a lawyer for help on whether he thinks a strike-out application could be worth making. If you succeed you get your costs back and lay down a powerful marker to the claimant.

(3) DISCONTINUANCE

If you want to drop your case before it is allocated you will have to pay your opponent's legal costs of defending the claim. These costs could stretch back to before the proceedings were issued and so it could be a larger bill than you realise. If you discontinue before your claim is allocated to the "small claims" track, be under no illusions – your opponent, if they are represented, will hunt you down for their costs, even though you do not feel this is fair. You will then have a fight on your hands and a possible court hearing to get a judge to rule otherwise.

This is a good example of why civil litigation is so much to do with tactics and the dangers of costs. Even though you may feel you have a good case not to have to pay, the practical problems of having to fight and get your case heard may well cause you to back down, perhaps agreeing with your opponent to pay a reduced amount of their costs. I go into discontinuance in more detail in the section of the Civil Procedure Rules below, with a real-life example.

(4) UNREASONABLE CONDUCT

Finally, even if it is allocated to the small claims track there is a common misconception that you never get your legal costs back if you win, but this does not always apply in every case. You also get back your court fees, expert fees, expenses, and time out of work if you win. (See CPR 27.14 and note the limits on experts' fees.) But legal costs can also be awarded where a loser has behaved *unreasonably*, at the judge's discretion.

On the fast track and multi-track, you can also get the court to award you a higher proportion of your costs, on what is called an "indemnity" rather than "standard" basis, if your opponent has conducted the litigation unreasonably.

So, to conclude, I encourage clients to think of their claim initially as simply a claim. You should not think it is a small claim, fast track claim, or multi-track claim - or any other sort of claim. Until it is actually allocated it is just a claim. You cannot elect from the outset that it be a small claim or a fast track claim. Although the procedure is slightly more relaxed for small claims (there is not a disclosure phase in the proceedings for example), it still takes place in front of the same judge who applies the same basic substantive law and the same basic procedural law. The substantive law means the cause of action – whether it is a claim in contract, misrepresentation, negligence, etc. You need to demonstrate that you have properly made out your cause of action in your claim, without which you will never get the plane off the ground. (I cover causes of action later.) The same law of the land applies whether your claim is £500 or £5,000,000, just as the same laws of aerodynamics and the same basis flying skills apply whether you are at the controls of a Boeing 747 or a single prop, Piper Alpha.

That being said, the vast majority of low-value claims of well under £10,000 will be allocated to the small claims track. If your claim is a simple, low-value claim, then read Chapter 3, which addresses the way in which these small claims work and the differences between the small claims and other tracks. Much of the other sections of this book will still be relevant, save for disclosure, and the sections on legal costs and certain special rules, such as the rules governing Part 36 offers, which you can probably skip.

The Civil Procedure Rules ("CPR")

Now let us turn to the rule book. It is easily accessible online and has about 90 Parts and nearly as many "Practice Directions" on top.

The woolliness around the small claims track mentioned above reflects the idiosyncrasies of the English legal system generally. Unfortunately, the English legal system is not a system of certainty. It is full of qualifications, caveats, variations, discretionary powers...and uncertainties! A lot of the CPR rules often finish with a nice little subsection at the end of each main section saying something like this: "But the judge can exercise his discretion to do anything he wants"! Continentals with their legal system would go crazy trying to work in ours. Our system is from the grassroots up and all vague, whilst theirs is top-down and arbitrary (to make a gross generalisation).

This is quite good for the litigant in person because he can appeal to an overarching principle of injustice or unfairness if a rule looks likely to trip them up. In fact, Part 1 of the Civil Procedure Rules pretty much says, "but none of these rules applies if it is unfair and unjust." In my experience, it is better to step back from your case and look at the headline principles rather than get lost in the details of the CPR. You could do worse if you are running your case than familiarise yourself with Part 1:

THE OVERRIDING OBJECTIVE - PART 1.1

> *(1) These Rules are a new procedural code with the overriding objective of enabling the court to deal with cases justly and at proportionate cost.*

> *(2) Dealing with a case justly and at proportionate cost includes, so far as is practicable –*

(a) *ensuring that the parties are on an equal footing;*
(b) *saving expense;*
(c) *dealing with the case in ways which are proportionate –*
    (i) *to the amount of money involved;*
    (ii) *to the importance of the case;*
    (iii) *to the complexity of the issues; and*
    (iv) *to the financial position of each party;*

(d) *ensuring that it is dealt with expeditiously and fairly;*
(e) *allotting to it an appropriate share of the court's resources, while taking into account the need to allot resources to other cases; and*
(f) *enforcing compliance with rules, practice directions and orders.*

The last one is a bit annoying. This is the need to know about the existence of the Civil Procedure Rules as a litigant in person and occasionally needing to refer to them! But the judge and the lawyer for the other side should help you understand and apply them– and will help you – provided you have not been stupid about ignoring them. Which is just as well, because trying to figure them out is a bit like trying to make sense of those technical books, like a Haynes Car Manual or a book on electrical wiring. It is not for the faint-hearted. Even a lot of lawyers have no clue what is going on, especially those who flirt with a civil litigation practice but are in reality non-contentious lawyers who are more experienced in dealing with buying houses and drafting wills. A little knowledge is a dangerous thing.

In spite of me "dissing" the rules, they can be incredibly helpful, because what you have to understand is that a judge will be almost paranoid about making sure he has obeyed them. This means that provided you can find something in the Civil Procedure Rules to support your position they will have to take you seriously whenever you are making a certain point, whether on paper or in court. So for those of you who want to go deeper into the procedural law to gain an advantage over your opponent, here is a 5-minute law school on the subject...

How to think like a lawyer?

Let's take a couple of examples in practice. Civil litigation is all about costs, so let's look at the unreasonable conduct provision we touched on earlier in respect of small claims. You may have thought that costs could not be awarded in respect of a small claim.[8] If you go to section 27.14 you will see a section on just this issue.

COSTS ON THE SMALL CLAIMS TRACK 27.14

(1) This rule applies to any case which has been allocated to the small claims track unless paragraph (5) applies.
(Rules 46.11 and 46.13 make provision in relation to orders for costs made before a claim has been allocated to the small claims track)

(2) The court may not order a party to pay a sum to another party in respect of that other party's costs, fees and expenses, including those relating to an appeal, except –
   (a) the fixed costs attributable to issuing the claim which –
      (i) are payable under Part 45; or
      (ii) would be payable under Part 45 if that Part applied to the claim;

   (b) in proceedings which included a claim for an injunction or an order for specific performance a sum not exceeding the amount specified in Practice Direction 27 for legal advice and assistance relating to that claim;
   (c) any court fees paid by that other party;
   (d) expenses which a party or witness has reasonably incurred in travelling to and from a hearing or in staying away from home for the purposes of attending a hearing;

---

8   If you google, "Civil Procedure Rules small claims track" you will find everything you need in Part 27.

(e) a sum not exceeding the amount specified in Practice Direction 27 for any loss of earnings or loss of leave by a party or witness due to attending a hearing or to staying away from home for the purposes of attending a hearing;

(f) a sum not exceeding the amount specified in Practice Direction 27 for an expert's fees;

(g) such further costs as the court may assess by the summary procedure and order to be paid by a party who has behaved unreasonably; and

(h) the Stage 1 and, where relevant, the Stage 2 fixed costs in rule 45.18 where –

  (i) the claim was within the scope of the Pre-Action Protocol for Low Value Personal Injury Claims in Road Traffic Accidents ('the RTA Protocol') or the Pre-action Protocol for Low Value Personal Injury (Employers' Liability and Public Liability) Claims ('the EL/PL Protocol');

  (ii) the claimant reasonably believed that the claim was valued at more than the small claims track limit in accordance with paragraph 4.1(4) of the relevant Protocol; and

  (iii) the defendant admitted liability under the process set out in the relevant Protocol; but

  (iv) the defendant did not pay those Stage 1 and, where relevant, Stage 2 fixed costs; and

(i) in an appeal, the cost of any approved transcript reasonably incurred.

The first thing to note is that subsection 2 says:

(2) The court may not order a party to pay a sum to another party in respect of that other party's costs, fees and expenses, except...

Note the word, "except". "What?! Exceptions?!" I hear you cry. Yes, and it lays out a few, such as court fees, expert fees, travelling expenses, and even loss of earnings for time spent at court.

So it looks as if you will not have to pay any costs if you lose your claim, doesn't it? But you have to read the whole section carefully, I am afraid. If you go down to section "g" you get this delightful caveat to everything that has just been said, because it allows the court to order:

g) such further costs as the court may assess...

What on earth does this mean!? The section goes on to say the judge can order these costs against a party who has behaved unreasonably.

In practice judges rarely do. But there is no harm in asking for additional costs if you can persuade a judge that your opponent has just been playing around, for example, by deliberately fighting a claim to make life difficult without there ever being prospects of winning. This *could* be unreasonable. As I say, it is unusual for judges to award costs but you may as well be the exception.

The problem is that litigants in person do not even think they can ask, because they have read on an online site or blog that you cannot get them in small claims. Also, they tend to be exhausted after the main trial and are so pleased with having won that they completely forget to claim their costs. And yet costs are the most important thing because, after all, this is a commercial endeavour in which you are claiming for your losses and those include costs.[9] So always ask for your costs! The judge can only say, "No."

Let's look at another example that I also alluded to earlier. I occasionally find clients asking me what to do in order to discontinue a claim they have already issued, perhaps because they are intimidated by a really good defence and the danger of costs of a represented party.

So what happens when people discontinue their claims? Do they have to pay their opponent's costs? Again, it is worth making a proper analysis of the rules before deciding to discontinue it. Typing in "civil procedure rules discontinuance" into Google should show you results like "Part 38 DISCONTINUANCE" or something like it. There will be a grey box at the top with sections and the one you want is "liability for costs". Click on it and see how it takes you right there:

---

9   See Chapter 2 of the book for an explanation of the importance of costs and Chapters 7 & 8 for more on costs' tactics and how to prepare a schedule of costs for hearings.

CPR 38.6

(1) Unless the court orders otherwise[10], a claimant who discontinues is liable for the costs which a defendant... incurred

But is this true of all claims, even claims allocated to the small claims track? Well, the answer is only a couple of sections below the above section, and it says,

(3) This rule does not apply to claims allocated to the small claims track.

Phew! So you're safe.
Or are you?
Well, think about the wording of the above: "allocated to the small claims track." So if your claim has not yet been officially allocated you will be liable for their costs!

So do you see the importance of tactics here? Having informed yourself about the law of procedure in this area you now know only to discontinue after the claim has been allocated. Only then you are safe in a small claim. Once again, you see the importance of waiting to make sure your claim is a small claim? The timing of discontinuance is critical.

If you are so minded and like the cut and thrust of the law of procedure (bless you) you can get some useful nuggets from the CPR quite easily without having to necessarily use a lawyer. It's just a case of drilling into the details a little bit and then reaping the rewards. You could just have saved yourself £2,500 adverse fees - not unusual for an opponent who has a lawyer at the point at which you discontinue. All because you read the CPR and now have realised you can wait a couple of months for the court to officially allocate, and only then discontinue.

There is no point trying to explain all of the rules to you. Better to just refer to the headline principles in CPR Part 1, if in doubt. But hopefully the above gives you a little bit of practical knowledge about the skills

---

10 Note how once more the court gives the judge the final say to do what he wants: "unless the court orders otherwise".

you need to apply if any technical issues relating to the rules come up – and how you can use them to your advantage.

The County Courts of England & Wales

So much for the rule book, what about the actual system? What is it like being up there in the air in this rarefied atmosphere? I guess that the lawyers are like the pilots who routinely fly and so are familiar with all the conditions – rain, fog, wind, storms, lightning, and turbulence and they know how to deal with it from experience. So let me give you the benefit of my experience.

The truth is that in the county court (the lower civil courts in which the vast majority of claims are handled) system is old-fashioned and the court underfunded. For instance, it might be very difficult to talk to someone on the phone. You might get routed through a call centre, which is not desired because you need to speak to a member of staff at the local court where your case has been listed, not a call centre which ends up being a barrier between you and someone who can help. There is often a huge variation between local courts, as some are better organised than others.

You also have to be aware of court fees. The courts do not do anything without money these days, and will just send your papers back completely unread unless you have paid a court fee first. This, I guess, is the government's solution to funding problems– to make the parties pay for the system. It is also a reflection of the times in which we live, that every transaction in life attracts a fee. The courts are no different. But paying a court can be complicated. The best way is sending an old-fashioned cheque made out to H.M.C.T.S. (Her Majesty's Courts and Tribunal Service.) If you opt to pay over the phone you have to write in and give the court a phone number to call you on and the times when you can be called. You then have to wait for a court officer to call you. If you are not in they may stop trying and then the court fee never gets taken and your papers never get read.

You also need to make sure to file and serve ("serve" means send to your opponent) all documents and you need to make sure that you label emails and letters correctly. There is guidance, often in the footer of the email sent by the courts as to what to put in the subject box, etc. If you do not correctly label them they might ignore you. Also, be aware that if you are filing electronically you must not go over a certain number of megabytes. If you do, again it gets rejected. I guess this is so their system is not clogged up. Do not forget, the problem here is that the court has to print out the documents to give to the judge. I had a case where my client was on the wrong end of a strike-out application because he did not use PDF format for his documents and so missed a court deadline.

My advice to people is to use old fashioned post if they are uncomfortable with email filing! In this way, you will know what the documents will look like when the judge gets them. And even then, I also recommend you bring extra copies of everything to court hearings and simply assume that the court will have lost them or not processed them in time. I usually choose one or the other and stick with it, because courts get angry when you file by email and post.

You are working against the grain, not with it, where county courts are concerned. You have to hold the courts by the hand and lead, especially if you are the claimant, because at law you have the main responsibility of managing the case. This also means regularly and routinely chasing the parties concerned instead of waiting for things to happen in this 20th-century bureaucratic system.

LEGAL ACCOUNTANT VS A SOLICITOR

I had a bad experience of this in a case in which we were acting on behalf of a legal accountant and suing a solicitor for unpaid invoices. The court was Clerkenwell & Shoreditch. Whilst we ultimately won the case, the length of the proceedings was ridiculous, stretching to beyond 18 months from the date of issue. The solicitor knew how to work the system and did not want to pay our client's invoices and so constructed a defence and counterclaim alleging our client was negligent. This led to complicated hearings, disclosure issues, and the need to instruct a legal accounting expert. All for a claim that had started out as a small claim of £10,000. (This is also a good example of a claim that looks like a simple small claim of chasing unpaid invoices but is allocated to a higher track.)

Court processing of documents was so poor that you hardly knew, at the time you turned up for a hearing, whether the judge would have anything remotely resembling what you thought you had sent in. I resorted to sending everything by recorded delivery as I was worried the court may have not been printing things out from email, or not printing them out accurately. I marked letters in bold with "urgent" and put the dates and details of hearings on the letters, such as saying, in capitals and bold at the top of the letter, "FOR HEARING ON 14 NOVEMBER 2019. URGENT".

Our opponent was a robust litigator running her own small practice and she would try and get hearings "vacated" (cancelled), alleging they were unnecessary as an agreed outcome could be sent into the court by means of what is called a "consent order". She did this because it ultimately just stretched out proceedings for longer and caused my client more emotional upset and made her wait for her money. She was trying to wear my client down and get her to throw the towel in. In cases like this, you really need to get as many hearings as possible, in order to get a judge to properly look your opponent in the eye.

I actually on one occasion instructed a specialist outdoor clerk to take papers to court for a hearing and to keep a total note of what had happened and make sure she actually got the judge to take the papers from her hands. It was infuriating how our opponent was able to play on the problems and stretch out the case for longer than it needed to be – and incur my client in additional legal costs of her lawyers having to manage the court system. Costs which she would never be able to recover because of the laws on "proportionality" (read on).

ONLINE COURTS

There are some rays of hope, however.

You can now use Money Claims Online (MCOL) for many cases. This is a centralised system, based in Northampton, through which you can issue and defend a claim entirely online – including paying the court fees. It can work very well for simple claims for a clear amount of money (specified money claims for less than £100,000) and if it becomes a long and complicated case it will be referred to a court where you can go over to paper or stay with email filing.[11] As lawyers, we do not use it much, but more often find ourselves taking over cases that have been started online but have become more complex.

Money Claims Online does not accept all types of claims and you should check whether your case fits a category of claim they are currently handling by going onto their website.

The courts are now also piloting a new system called, "Online Civil Claims Pilot" which will run until late 2021. This is only for claims under £10,000 and the details of it are covered in the Civil Procedure Rules at Practice Direction 51R. Check the Practice Direction for a large number of exceptions (for example, it cannot be used for personal injury claims). Initial feedback suggests it can be quicker and defendants are more responsive. So, for simple money claims and debt recovery claims it might be worth trying.

KEY FACTORS

These are the key factors that you need to be aware of when dealing with the county courts:

(1) **Proportionality of Claim**. The County Court system has limited resources and will allocate accordingly. The truth is that a small claim may need as much work as a large claim. Take the example of a second hand Ford Fiesta compared to a Lamborghini. In both claims, you might have been mis-sold a damaged car and so need to set out your claim in the same way and with the same amount of evidence and probably even the same expert, and yet

---

11 Some solicitors do not accept service by email and you have to post them a letter in order to properly serve them! They still live in the dark ages.

one claim is valued at £5,000 and the other at £100,000. One gets allocated to small claims and one gets allocated to multi-track. There are huge differences: the ability to get your legal costs if you win in the case of the Lamborghini, increased court involvement, having to spend far more time on disclosure, statements, experts, and the trial itself (which will be 2 days as opposed to ½ day long). It seems unfair because for some people a £5,000 claim is as serious as a £100,000 claim is to a richer person.

(2) Proportionality of Costs. Just as the court's involvement will be reduced on a lower track, so they will expect costs to be lower. This will be lawyers fees, experts' fees, time spent on the case and so on.[12] All these costs will be judged against a yardstick of "proportionality". Even if they are reasonable costs they will still be discounted unless they are also "proportionate". So a low-value legal accounting negligence claim cannot justify expensive lawyers and extensive use of court time and hearings. But the same case, had it been worth £100,000 rather than £10,000, would justify a greater amount of costs, even though it may be based on very similar facts and require the same amount of work in terms of statements of case, disclosure issues, witnesses and so on. Arguably, once again, this may mean that you do not get full access to justice merely because the value of your claim is lower.

(3) Case Management. You need to lead the court by the hand. As I have said, this includes being totally on top of filing and serving paperwork and paying attention to small details, such as filing documents and emails correctly and ensuring that documents arrive with court staff in ample time for hearings and deadlines. You have to read the small print of the court's directions on how to file, since there are very precise requirements in the email signature of each court, such that if you do not comply documents may simply never get to the judge. This is covered in greater detail in Chapters 2 and 4.

---

12 Litigants in Person can also claim back money for their own time spent on a case. See Part 6 of this book.

(4) Hearings. If you are a claimant, you have to make the most of hearings in front of a judge, who is focused there and then. It is common sense. Nothing gets done without a hearing and if a defendant who has decided to just ignore your claim and stick their head in the sand is forced to turn up in person, that will focus their minds fabulously. In a way, a hearing, even a ten minute one, is just so important in getting matters organised. Conversely, my advice to a defendant would be to try and get a claimant to agree to vacate hearings so that they are forced into a long-game. In other words, use the slow and underfunded court system to get their claim kicked into the long-grass and constantly harp on about how the amount of work the claimant is doing is "disproportionate" for such a low-value claim.

(5) Preparation of Particulars of Claim: "By failing to prepare you are preparing to fail."[13] You are holding yourself out as a hostage to fortune if you do not get your claim properly prepared beforehand and issued correctly. This is what happened in the legal accountant's case I gave as a case study. She just felt very annoyed about the solicitor giving her the runaround and not paying invoices and so "banged off" a claim. She ran into a problematic court with a claim that was full of errors. She tried and failed to get it allocated to the small claims track. Ultimately, the fact she only instructed us to run the proceedings *after* the pre-action phase made it incredibly expensive for her because she had to amend her claim and deal with all sorts of disclosure issues and a negligence counterclaim during proceedings.[14] That could have been avoided if she had properly prepared her case (or paid lawyers to do so) before issuing and made sure her claim was in apple-pie order.

(6) Limited Legal Advice. If in doubt and your claim is of high enough value to justify the expense, use lawyers on a limited basis for

---

13 Quote by Benjamin Franklin.
14 In other words, the plane was up in the air and she was burning money. Have you ever heard of someone trying to repair a plane in mid-air? Even re-fuelling is a pretty expensive business.

some fixed fee advice early on.[15] I cover the ways in which you can get the best value from a lawyer and make them work for you and not the other way around in chapter 6 of this book.

The best way to use lawyers if you are representing yourself in court is at the pre-issue stage and at the time you issue. You can then fly the plane yourself in the knowledge that the aeroplane has been properly maintained, checked, inspected and authorised by the control tower and taken-off from the correct runway into the correct air corridor. Flying the plane once it is in the air is much easier. Indeed, pilots used to let passengers come into the cockpit decades past and even take the controls. My father did this with me in his single-prop Piper Alpha plane. But, he never let me take off!

Also note that some lawyers will do "No Win No Fee" so that you only pay their legal bill if you win, which could be a good option for limiting your costs exposure (in return you part with some of your winnings). However, they will only do this for fast-track and multi-track claims. That being said, the system is evolving and there is now a new type of retainer[16] called a "Damages-Based Agreement". Some lawyers should be prepared to enter into this for small track claims at the upper end of the £10,000 threshold. I cover these types of contingency agreements in detail in Chapter 6.

IMPORTANCE OF ORGANISATION

Do not be discouraged by the antiquated court system, rather simply play it to your advantage. Be more organised than your opponent. If you have acquired some knowledge on the way civil litigation works and have an understanding of the Civil Procedure Rules you will, in fact, be head and shoulders above your opponent, especially if they are not represented. Even if they are, this can sometimes be a tactical advantage as they will be spending a lot of money on running the litigation, whereas you will be running it yourself and so keeping your costs down. This means you could win the costs battle in the long-run, costs being the ever-present "spectre" in the background of most fast and multi-track claims.

---

15 Not later, when it becomes more expensive and is less effective.

16 A retainer is the term for your engagement letter or letter of instruction, which all lawyers should provide you with at the outset, even if only an email with standard terms attached.

DOG'S DINNER

Recently I had a high-value claim where I was acting for the defendant, a businessman. He owed a large amount of money to the claimant but the claimant's solicitors made a dog's dinner of the claim particulars (sadly, solicitors get it wrong pretty often too). This was a case where there was complexity because the loan was secured against a property and they used the wrong procedure. (They had not read the CPR carefully.)

Not only did the claimant not win their case, but because they had messed up they had to discontinue the entire proceedings and as I write are locked into costs proceedings. These are an entirely separate set of pro-ceedings. It has taken nearly half a year to decide how much they now have to pay the defendant for the legal costs he incurred in defending a badly brought claim! (£13,000 costs.) Worse, the claimant cannot go back to court with fresh proceedings and have a second bite at the cherry until they have settled our costs or had these costs proceedings decided by a specialist costs judge. This is taking a very long time to get listed and heard. (I made sure of that.) This is even where they have a strong case on the substantive, main claim.

If you are a defendant you can really run rings around a claimant who has not followed protocol and procedure. You can make them angry, frustrated and indignant, which just results in them losing perspective on their case and making errors, as my opponent solicitor in the example above has done. This makes the proceedings way more expensive for them in comparison to settling out of court.

SPECIALIST COURTS

Finally, if you have a large or complex claim like a contested will or an intellectual property claim, you will likely not use the County Court System at all, but higher, specialist courts such as the High Court,

Chancery Court or the Intellectual Property & Enterprise Court (IPEC). If that is you, a lot of the problems I have mentioned above will disappear! Some of these are great courts where you can actually get to talk to the person managing the cases, the judge's clerk. Still, if you are reading this book – on the small claims track, fast track, or multi-track - you will almost certainly be in the good old County Court, I am afraid.

Can a Litigant in Person succeed?

You might be right to ask the question, "Do I really want to get involved in the court system at all? Is it wise to run my claim, especially a multi-track claim?" I think the answer to this question is that you do have to pick your battles in life. You should not end up in the courts more than once or twice in a life-time – once is enough, to be honest. But just that once or twice you will need to stand up for yourself.

Before I was a lawyer this happened to me. I was contemplating a career in the film industry. I had made a short film and lent the editor £2,000 to upgrade his editing equipment. There was more editing work than he had envisaged and he felt short-changed by the price he had agreed. And so somehow during the editing of the movie he decided that £500 was not enough and that he needed to dip into the loan monies. But a deal is a deal. He then refused to repay the loan.

I issued my claim and the matter was allocated to the small claims track, as it was clearly a simple low-value claim that the small claims track is designed for. He fought all the way but then did not turn up for the trial and I got a judgment against him. He paid up. So, it was a successful decision. And that is the only time I have ever litigated a dispute of my own.

So the system does work, even though the court process is not perfect; subject to delays, bureaucratic errors and unnecessary expense. I also think that for a small business it is important to learn about how the courts work because it will make you more confident as a businessman to have a little knowledge about the legal system.

But you do have to bear in mind my general point about seeing the process of going to court as an entrepreneurial endeavour that has come about, off the back of a cold-headed commercial decision that the rewards justify the risk. Fighting battles for the sake of principles, for the sake of "honour", is the province of the wealthy and such battles should only very occasionally be fought by private individuals and small businesses. Discretion is the better part of valour. But occasionally, probably increasingly in this day and age, you will find people who try it on and you do then need to act with conviction and with purpose and drag them kicking and screaming to court.

You may also worry that your opponent will not have the money to pay the judgement even if you win.[17] Remember, you can always urge a repayment plan on the court and they will probably go for it. The issue here will be for you to provide evidence to the court as to their income, as they will doubtless try and hide this when it comes to filling in the court forms. Unpaid loans are commonplace in terms of county court proceedings. Last year I had a case where my client had lent £5,000 to his personal trainer as capital for her business, she had not paid it back and so he ran his claim in the courts – it was allocated to the small claims track. He just used me judiciously, to help with limited advice on key areas. He got a judgment against her and managed to get her on a repayment plan of £200 odd a month.

What if you are up against an opponent who is represented? Don't worry. The courts are very sympathetic to litigants in person and actually, an opponent's lawyer is meant to help you as they have a duty not just to their client but also the court. I often see judges bending over backwards to accommodate litigants in person and it can almost be a positive advantage, especially where your opponent is having to burn money on lawyers but you are not. This gives you a tactical advantage. Courts will overlook minor errors and missed court deadlines and won't be too strict about applying the Civil Procedure Rules. I should not have to say this, but it is a fact.

However, before you get too comfortable, read below...

---

17 See a later section on Enforcement for more detail on this.

What happens if I do not comply with the Civil Procedure Rules?

The important thing to understand is that you are unlikely to have your case thrown out if you do not comply with court orders and the civil procedure rules, because in practice a judge is likely to be sympathetic to a litigant in person and he can always make a costs order against you for a specific failure in the proceedings or if your opponent is forced to do extra work because of your breach.[18]

So, in fact, although you will not get your case thrown out, you may well find yourself on the wrong end of a costs order. So costs are the real danger. You see, instead of preventing a case from going forward (which might be considered unjust and unfair), the judge can punish you with costs. Making costs orders is the usual way for a court to deal with transgressions. Although even then my experience is that the judge is only likely to use costs orders against a litigant in person if they have messed up at least more than once.[19]

In practice a single judge, in a busy county court stretched thin in terms of resources, simply does not have time to look into the matter in any detail and is so afraid of making a wrong judgment against a litigant in person. Throughout a piece of litigation, many different judges will be involved in your case – it is not just allocated to one judge throughout. So whilst "ignorance of the law is no defence", in practice ignorance of the procedural law is! To a point. At least for litigants in person.

The difference comes if it ever gets to trial or a long and important interim hearing of some sort. So in the legal account's case, I have referred to when we finally "got her" at a two-hour disclosure hearing that had been specially listed to deal with her flagrant breach of court orders. The judge had read the case properly and gave her a roasting and ordered costs against her. Afterwards, the claim was settled. It takes

---

18 After every interim hearing, a judge will talk to the parties about costs, after having dealt with the main business of the hearing. People forget about this, but it is such an important feature of civil litigation. See Part 7 section 4 on these issues and the importance of schedules of costs.

19 I often find myself tearing my hair out at how indulgent judges are to litigants in person who break the rules, not even making a costs order against them.

a hearing like this to get a person to sober up and accept reasonable settlement proposals.

Ultimately, whilst in the knockabout world of the county court system you can get away with a lot and string a case out for ages, you do have to be careful and direct this remark particularly at the defendants out there, I would not advise you to get into the habit of breaching court rules and not complying with the CPR.[20]

This is because the courts have recently clarified that they should not deal with litigants in person differently and give them special treatment because of the complexity of the rules. There have been recent cases in 2019, culminating in one case where a litigant in person did not serve documents on their opponent's solicitor by post by a certain deadline. But they had sent them by email. Unfortunately, however, the order required service by post. So here was a technical breach. Did the appeal court let them off? No, I am afraid not. It was decided that the courts should only make concessions to litigants in person in respect of the Civil Procedure Rules where they were very "obscure" or difficult to penetrate but explained this as the exception rather than the rule. The current climate is, therefore, not to make a special exception for litigants in person on account of the complexity of the CPR.

A trial or an important interim hearing, in front of a judge who has read all the papers, is often the place where litigants in persons get a rude awakening. They have lived in their little bubble the entire case and feel indignant and angry about matters and have ignored sensible attempts to settle and reasonable – commercially sensible - offers. Everyone always thinks that their point of view is the right one when more often than not there are shades of grey. They end up bristling, ready for battle, and then, much to their surprise, get a thumping. Often simply because they never stood back and made a realistic appraisal of their case. Then they find themselves with a double-whammy of a costs order against them for their opponent's legal costs, perhaps even as much as the claim value itself.

So, in reality, the biggest danger for you, if you are a litigant in person, is not being realistic about your case and not taking a commercial view, weighing the costs of proceedings against the benefit of negotiating

---

20 I am simply saying "do not worry" if you make a slip here or there.

and accepting a low offer. As I repeatedly will mention throughout this book, civil litigation must be seen in the same way you would a business – does the continued expenditure on costs and lost time justify the potential upside of a win?

General Form of Judgment or Order	In the County Court at Clerkenwell & Shoreditch

Claim Number	
Date	8 October 2019

	1st Claimant Ref
	1st Defendant Ref

Before Deputy District Judge Woodcraft sitting at the County Court at Clerkenwell & Shoreditch, The Gee Street Courthouse, 29-41 Gee Street, London, EC1V 3RE.

Upon hearing the Claimant in person and hearing the Representative for the Defendant

IT IS ORDERED THAT

1. Judgment for Claimant against Defendant for: £2756.02 (including interest) and costs of £285.00 (including witness expenses) = total £3,041.02
2. To be paid on or before 17 November 2019

Dated 26 September 2019

The court office at the County Court at Clerkenwell & Shoreditch, The Gee Street Courthouse, 29-41 Gee Street, London, EC1V 3RE. When corresponding with the court, please address forms or letters to the Court Manager and quote the claim number. Tel: 02072 507200 Fax: 0870 761 7688. Check if you can issue your claim online. It will save you time and money. Go to www.moneyclaim.gov.uk to find out more.

N24 General Form of Judgment or Order

Produced by: G Jama
CJR065C

Let's conclude this section with an upbeat tale. As I was writing the first draft of this book and quite recently, I got a great email from someone who had been watching some of the free videos on my YouTube channel and wanted to thank me for the help. The videos had got him through a difficult small claim against an opponent who was legally backed. He even attached the judgement - £3,000 plus costs! He had done it completely without paying any lawyers, just using the materials provided by us for free online. He was a smart guy. It was a very moving email and endorsement of the fact that a person can master it on their own. It even made me teary-eyed to think that someone was so grateful for the benefit of the endless hours I had spent making the videos. Here is the actual judgment (names redacted):

Legal Resources

So, apart from this book and the videos that we do on the Redwood Legal's YouTube channel, where can you and free legal help?

Legal Aid. It was created over 60 years ago, in a time when it was seen as an important plank of the welfare state. There was a time when you could get legal aid for quite a wide range of disputes but in line with the general move to saving money and cutting budgets legal aid has been substantially removed Along with Legal Aid cuts, publicly funded or charitable law advice centres that had benefited from Legal Aid, such as The Citizens Advice Bureau, has been seriously cut.[21] Legal Aid is now only available for areas like crime, discrimination, abuse, care including childcare cases, harassment, domestic violence, asylum, mental health and these sorts of exceptional areas. I doubt this is an area of dispute for you if you are reading this book.

Fee Remission. It is worth remembering that Legal Aid can help you with fee remission if you are on a low enough income. This means you would avoid having to pay what are increasingly high legal fees for issuing a claim and paying other court fees.

The Citizens Advice Bureau. In spite of the cuts, the Citizens Advice Bureau is a good resource, certainly online. For instance, in their Small

---

21 The number of law centres has halved from 94 in 2013/14 to 47 in July 2019 since the Legal Aid, Sentencing and Punishment of Offenders Act removed vast swaths of civil law from the scope of public funding in 2013.

Claims section, you will find a breakdown of the process of going to court and there are even templates, for example, a letter that you should write before bringing legal proceedings. There are also useful links to relevant sites, like the Ministry Of Justice's site and the Money Claims Online site, where you can make your claim electronically. In terms of advice over the phone, there are limitations as advisers can not stray into giving you tailored legal advice on the facts of your particular case, but merely general advice about the law and procedure. This is still helpful of course, but do not have overly high expectations of the extent to which they can advise you about your specific case.

Incidentally, there are also other charities online offering legal advice and help. I guess that now, whilst legal aid is being stripped down to the bone, this sort of free help will now become the province of philanthropists and charitable donations. One example of such a service would be "Law Works" at www.lawworks.org.uk. They are targeted at those who are not eligible for legal aid, nevertheless cannot afford a lawyer and people who want to know whether they ought to instruct a lawyer or not.

Bar Pro Bono Unit, Advocate, Free Representation Unit. The service works by finding a junior barrister, who is not yet fully qualified, to represent you at hearings for free. These services operate in the same field. I was a member of the Free Representation Unit when I was qualifying as a barrister and I represented clients in social security and employment claims. These are the main areas that these services can help you with. Barristers are keen to get advocacy experience and so you can often find decent help there, certainly in the areas I mention.

Legal Expenses Insurance. You may have insurance to help you pay legal fees without realising. More often than not people do not even realise that they do as it might have been sold alongside some other insurance. It may have looked cheap and you might have, therefore, ticked the box for it alongside your car or home insurance. I rarely find it works, however, I am speaking from my own experience. You will certainly need to read the small print very carefully, as it will have exclusions, caps and may be limited to only certain types of cases or stages of proceedings. It may also require you to use a particular lawyer from a list of approved lawyers and thus not allow you to choose the one you want.

Consumer Help Sites. Money Saving Expert is a well-known website in this area and whilst it deals primarily with finance matters it also has a section on small claims that is very good. However, as with any website, information can be out of date and so you need to be careful with these types of sites. When searching the website I discovered an error on their site in relation to a change in court fees and found that they also oversimplify matters sometimes. I do not like, for instance, the way they describe the Small Claims Track as the Small Claims Court: this is the problem I alluded to earlier and makes people think they can elect to go to a specific, stand-alone court with their claim.

Claims Companies. This is a controversial area. I have dealt with claims companies over my time; the good, the bad and the ugly. This was especially the case when I was working in the area of payment protection insurance litigation. Whilst I do not have a problem with a company that takes away the headache in return for a percentage of the winnings, I feel the danger is that if your claim is at all complex you might well be short-changed since the way these companies make money resembles a factory pushing exercise - taking as many claims through as possible and often taking the first (low) offer that comes along.

One thing you might want to do if you are considering using such firms is asking them whether they have a solicitor they can turn to in the case of complexity. This will show you whether or not they acknowledge, as a professional should, that some complex claims may need a lawyer.

Ombudsman Services. You can make a claim to the Financial Ombudsman Service if you have a financial complaint against a bank. In fact, in most financial claims against banks, you do need to use it first before going to court to demonstrate to the judge that you tried "alternative dispute resolution". If you are suing a lawyer, they have their own internal complaints procedure as well as the Legal Ombudsman Service, which will deal with the complaint if the law firm rejects it.

Books. I actually find that there are some really good books out there that can help you a lot better than some of the online sites. There is something about a book, with all the knowledge in a single tome that you can hold, feel and browse that means, especially in the area of law, they can prove invaluable. Student textbooks authored by reputable law schools or legal practitioners, whether produced for trainee barristers or solicitors, have to be clear, comprehensive and up to date and so can be relied upon. So whatever is being used at the LPC, the Legal Practice Course that trainee solicitors have to go on, is likely to be very reliable and also simpler and clearer than the books used by experienced practitioners. Likewise, whatever books trainee barristers at Bar School use.

Incidentally, the Judiciary has also introduced a Litigants in Person Practice Guide, but it is dated March 2013 and although a worthy tome I do wonder whether or not such efforts are now rapidly out of date.

Civil Procedure Rules. These rules are of course the ultimate bible and touchstone for all procedural issues in the civil courts (There are a whole different set for Family law, incidentally). There are Practice Directions alongside the rules, which should be read in conjunction with them. As they are available online and run by a government department they will be up to date.

"Unbundled" Services. This is the technical word for when a lawyer just gives you some very tailored or specific advice on a particular area.[22] I like to call such a service "Lawyer Lite". You should be able to access a one-hour legal surgery with a solicitor this way, or affordable fixed-fee work for specific, tailored advice. You might also get help in drafting documents or completing court forms. (Or even advocacy at court.) Prepare your documentation and a summary of the case and ask the lawyer to quote for the specific work you want to be done.

It is important to understand that the lawyer will not be conducting the litigation for you and running your case and is, therefore, only able to give advice based on the limited documentation you will provide. (For example, he might not really know the extent and strength of the case

---

22 I go into detail about this at the end of the book, in the section on tactics.

against you.) With 'Lawyer Lite" you are flying the plane but radioing into the control tower as necessary.

Due to the erosion of the welfare state and the increase in society's focus on money, coupled with the changes in the court rules, I believe that in the future there will be more and more litigants in person who will just use lawyers on an "as needed" basis.

Finally: make sure that any legal resource you do rely on is up to date!

Appendix

NO WIN NO FEE

I discussed retainers in the book and this type of particular retainer is important for litigants in person to be aware of. I have taken over cases that my clients have been running on their own and done it on a discounted or fully „no win no fee" basis. If you can get a lawyer to look at the possibility of a contingency arrangement, or "no win no fee", then this is very good – it may well be preferable than a traditional taxi meter rate, for obvious reasons. You will probably have to pay them to look at the case first so they form a view it is a strong one.

Above all „no win no fee" changes the relationship between you and the lawyer. It turns them into your business partner, which means they are highly incentivised to get a good result for you, rather than just letting the meter run. This is, therefore, a very good way of weeding out the conscientious lawyers from the gravy-train ones. You will have to pay them to look into your case initially, but once they feel it is strong they should at least be prepared for contingency or conditional fee arrangements.

Not all cases are suitable for contingency fee deals, but hopefully by the end of this section you will have got a handle on whether your case is. The basic reason for this is that it works only where there is a clear, identifiable pot of gold at the end of the case that a lawyer can leverage. This ensures that once the case is won there will be a guaranteed payment. For example, a property or an estate in a will dispute, or a big corporation who will not have difficulty finding the money.

NEGLIGENCE

Let's take an example that is based on a case I am currently running at time of writing. A client had asked us for preliminary advice on a £15,000 claim for which he paid £450 + VAT. At a later date he came back to us and wondered whether we would handle the entire case for him. He was finding the case against a very determined builder challenging. He was also exhausted from the fight and feeling he was just too close to his own case.

A lot of complexities had arisen around the negligence and there was a need to amend the claim. It transpired that a wall had been moved across a neighbour's property without planning consent. In other words, in light of the information, we needed to "beef up" the claim by an application to amend, using our old favourite, the N244.

We were able to offer him a 'no win no fee' deal for this, which we did at the disclosure phase. Because we had done that initial piece of advice and felt he had a strong case, we were happy to do this. When engaged we could also, of course, carefully calibrate a Part 36 offer, to boot – like launching a laser guided missile.

Any self-respecting law firm should do a review before it enters into a 'no win no fee' deal. It can be risky for a law firm not least because it can take so long until they see any money and need to cash flow a case. A law firm has to be convinced that it is a strong case. (The exception to this is the personal injury sector where large 'factory' firms can just "play the odds" and take on all sorts of cases.)

Tactically the use of 'no win no fee' retainers can be powerful and that is why I say any self-respecting law firm should be prepared to enter into them. It signals to your opponent that:

- ❖ A law firm specialising in litigation is now chasing them down;
- ❖ The law firm is hungry and are highly motivated to win as much as possible and as quickly as possible because they will not get paid until they do, and
- ❖ There may be a large legal bill that could double the costs of the whole proceedings if he were to lose.

So, here you can see how instructing a law firm can be a purely tactical decision. It is a little like radio-ing in an extra Spitfire against a particularly tricky Messerschmitt. He might suddenly turn tail and flee. And in this case the extra Spitfire has not cost you any extra money because he has agreed only to be paid if he wins – from a share of the spoils.

The Background

Over the past few decades the principle of proportionality of costs has led to a move in the direction of not just fixed fee regimes and budgets for running cases, but also towards "contingency" or "conditional" fee agreements. In 2013, the government expanded the 'no win no fee' regime and added a more American-like element which was the creation of what are called, "Damages-Based-Agreements". I am personally an advocate of them, if the case is right. What I like about them is that they turn the law firm into a business partner, rather than a taxi who just lets the meter run indefinitely. (On a trip where you do not know the destination or how long it will take!)

In contingency fee cases the lawyer does not get paid, or charges only a discounted rate, unless he gets you a result. Whether he gets paid or not is "contingent" on the result - in other words it depends on the outcome. Many law firms do not like them for this very reason. The additional problem is that you have to wait a long time for your money even if your case is successful. If you have ever run a business you will understand the adage that "cash is king". The value of cash now is worth ten times more than some possible cash that may come to you at some indefinite time in the future. And so lawyers do not like this arrangement. Fair enough. Cases can take years to reach court and even after victory there is the problem of recovery.

I should say, of course, that there are law firms that specialise in "no win no fee" exclusively. But this is usually limited to the personal injury sector.

I will give you a quick lesson in all of this and the short and dirty of the "skinny" on these contingency arrangements, which more properly deserve a book in their own right.

The Skinny on "No Win No Fee": The Treasure Island Analogy

I will use an analogy to try and explain how these complex types of retainers work. It applies in the ease of "no win no fee" or a "conditional fee agreement", something that we have had for the last 30 years.

Let's say you have a treasure map (a good case) but you need a skipper (the lawyer) to sail you to treasure island. You do not know how long the journey will take and how much it will cost. The skipper tells you his day rate for his ship and his crew and you nearly faint. So you say to him,

"Is there another way? It is a lot of treasure but I cannot afford your day rate right now as I am not made of money." And he says,

"Well, listen, I will do it for free, but once we do find the treasure I will charge you double my hourly rate, yes?"

Well, you see the sense in this but you might be worried just how big this figure is ultimately going to be. Let's say the island is thousands of miles away in the middle of the Pacific and it may take many months to get there. His day rate could be very large, even before it is doubled.

You say to him, "Okay, I see the sense in that, but what if your fees eat up all the treasure and there's nothing left for me? The whole exercise will be a bit pointless."

He says to you, "Good point. Okay, look. I will limit my fees to no more than 25% of your treasure. I will 'cap' my fees. But you are going to have to pick up costs along the way, expenses like port fees, navigator's costs and soldier's pay to protect us from any natives or cannibals on the island or pirates en route.[68] I am not going to pay for these. I have enough to pay for with my ship and my crew."

---

68 Court, expert, barrister's and insurance fees.

You can just about afford these expenses so you agree.

He might say to you, "25% is not enough as the treasure is not big and the journey long and risky. So I want a 50% cap."

Well, you might moan about this, but at the end of the day it is a business partnership, a deal, in which you are getting at least something, instead of nothing, all thanks to his help. You might say to him, "35%, but only if you help me pay these expenses if cash is tight."

And he says, "Okay, deal."

You can see how the amount of treasure (claim value) and the riskiness of the journey (the merits of the claim) are important factors in deciding what percentage to charge.

Now I have mentioned "expenses" above. You should be aware that there is no such thing as a free lunch. You are going to have to put your hand in your pocket to pay for court fees, counsel's advice, if needed, expert's fees and so on. You may also have to pay for "After the Event Insurance" - insurance which protects you from having to pay a large legal bill if you lose, where your opponent is instructed by expensive lawyers, for instance. This insurance pays out the premium in a lump-sum right at the end of the case if you lose and takes a part of your treasure if you win. It will have an up-front fee.

We now also have "damages-based agreements" (DBAs). These are American-style agreements, introduced in 2013.

Going back to the treasure island analogy, in this case the skipper says to you, "Okay, I will work entirely for free, <u>win or lose</u>, but I want 25% of the treasure. Period."

"What about your hourly rate?" you ask. "Aren't you going to charge me anything for all your time and expense?"

"Forget about that", he says. "I'll just do it for a share of the treasure." He then thinks for a minute, "In fact" he adds, "I will even pay all the expenses."

So you see that in the 'no win no fee' arrangement you have the lawyer double his hourly rate and use a cap to make sure his fees do not gobble up all the treasure, but in the case of DBAs, it is very simple – he just takes a share.

DBA sounds just like the ticket, right?

Well, yes, it works for you but does it work for the skipper?

Actually, in the case of the DBA he knows that particular island and he knows the size of the treasure and it is huge. So he is happy to take a risk.

Unfortunately most cases are not like this, and this is why very few skippers are going to agree to a DBA. Unless the claim value is very large - seven figures, let's say - the 'no win no fee' agreement is better for him in every way. This is because of the limitations that were brought in at the time they were introduced. Without boring you with the detail, the 2013 Act made some conditions around DBAs, which rather hamstrung the whole point of them! So that in most average cases lawyers do not touch them! The reason is that the old guard are afraid of our legal system turning into an American-style business market and so are very grudging and slow at changing the law. It will probably take further legislation to advance the process to make them fully-fledged contingency arrangements like they have in the US.

Having said all that, there is an area in which a lawyer may well consider DBAs and that is in small claims of high enough value. This is because you do not usually get your legal costs paid on that track so a CFA will not work, but a DBA with high enough value (let's say anything over £5,000) may be worth it, if they are getting at least 25%-50%. (50% is the limit, inclusive of VAT.) I offered to do one recently with a client who had already done a lot of work on his case.

You could view this as a case where the treasure is not big but the sea journey is very short, just a day's sailing across the bay. So the skipper thinks, "Yeah, why not? I've not got much on at the moment and my crew are bored."

As an alternative to both DBAs and CFAs, you could simply ask a lawyer to "cap" the amount of their legal fees. They would work on a traditional taxi meter arrangement but would agree to not go above a certain amount. For example, they would not go above £4,000 costs in any event in a £10,000 claim. Not many will, but there are enough exceptions to make it worth asking, and lawyers really do need to start moving with the times. There's no harm in asking! If I had a client who was super-organised with a straightforward claim I might well do this type of retainer.

You might also consider bringing in a lawyer half-way. A lot of clients actually do a really great job of initially bringing the claim but then get into choppy weather and suddenly realise they need help.

In that case, a lawyer can turn things around for you - if, after the initial hourly rate work he thinks you have a strong case, he may even do a 'no win no fee' at that point. Or you could just use him to strengthen your case and then drop him for the trial. It's like letting a pilot handle a bit of the journey after take off but before landing in a severe storm or fog whilst you do everything else. It does not stop you taking back the controls afterwards. You may only want to use him where it is essential.

In short, it is good as a litigant in person to have an experienced pilot to hand, who can take over the controls of the plane, if you feel it is necessary. As I said earlier, if a litigation law firm is not prepared to entertain CFAs or DBAs then you really do have to question whether they are properly equipped as a law firm to fight for their clients. If they say, "we don't do them", they are actually limiting your tactical options immediately and significantly, without a thought.

As litigators they should be trying to make sure that there are many options, or weapons, available to you as possible in order to get your claim over the wire. Their retainers can be a key weapon. Opponents facing lawyers who are on 'no win no fee' arrangements know that they are facing a tough opponent – they think the case is strong enough to take it on a contingency basis and will be more determined than the usual lawyers because they will not get paid until they win! A great move in some cases and a way of bringing them to the negotiating table.

To conclude, not all cases are suitable for 'no win no fee'. Where there is not a clear pile of treasure at the end of the journey, or something that can easily be converted into money - like a property or an estate in a will - they are less likely to be of use. To find out whether or not they are suitable, a lawyer is going to have to do some work initially. Sadly, there is no such thing as a "free lunch".

Finally, I should say that there are certain people who waste a lot of my time by phoning up and wanting to spend an hour talking about their case and saying, "This is a sure-fire winner. You need to do it on a 'no win no fee'. It's a great case I've got for you here!" That's nonsense. Not even a lawyer with his own dispute can think in a rational and detached way about its true merits.

You cannot assess a winner unless you have spent at least a couple of hours getting to know the case papers and the client. I have learned this the hard way from having wasted a lot of time on people's hopeless cases in the past. I have also learned that when someone tells me I should do a no win no fee because their claim is a sure-fire winner – this is a good indicator that it is a sure-fire dud.

GLOSSARY

After The Event Insurance: Used with no win no fee cases. This special insurance pays out your opponent's legal costs if you lose. It is usually only payable if you win using your winnings.

Allocation: The point, after statements of case, or pleadings, have been filed or served and is the decision of the court as to whether to send the claim down the small claims, fast, or multi-track. Directions Questionnaires are used to allocate. You can appeal an allocation decision and apply to re-allocate.

Alternative Dispute Resolution (ADR): The courts are big on people trying to settle disputes without going to court. This means any and all methods to achieve this, the most common of which is mediation. But, this also includes arbitration and the newly created, early neutral evaluation. It could also include a formal meeting, or even an online call or conference, whose purpose it is to try and reach a settlement.

Appeal: If you do not like the judgment you get at county court level, you can appeal. This appeal is still likely to be heard at a county court level. You have a strict time-frame in which to appeal and if you think it likely you should ask the judge after judgment for permission to appeal. If it is refused there is then a formal process to apply for leave to appeal.

Budgets: Courts are now big on parties estimating their legal costs of running a claim so that those costs can be kept proportionate and not be allowed to escalate unnecessarily. Thus, parties are required to budget what their costs are likely to be. In multi-track claims you have to complete a Precedent H, and even in fast-track claims a budget may be required by a court order. Litigants in person are not required to produce a Precedent H, but it may, at least, be a good idea to produce a short-form budget and also do not forget to challenge the amount of your opponent's Precedent H if they are represented by solicitors.

Civil Procedure Rules (CPR): The bible on how to run a civil claim. There are other rules for family cases. For personal injury, although they fall within the civil procedure rules, there are quite specific sections that apply to them and this can be complex. Do not forget there are also "Practice Directions" which should be read alongside the rules, to help people implement the rules properly.

Costs Schedules: Costs are a big feature of civil litigation and more important than in other areas of law. At any and every hearing you should be prepared to argue for your costs of that particular hearing if you win and at the end of the claim you should produce a schedule of your entire costs of the whole proceedings. Even if you lose, you might get some of your costs, for instance if you have made an offer early on that is better than your opponent's victory.

Conditional Fee Arrangement ("No Win no Fee"): This is basically a retainer with a solicitor where they are only paid if they actually win. In practice, you will have to find some money. For example, for the early stages when a solicitor is just reviewing your case on its merits and has not decided whether he will do no win no fee, or for disbursements like court fees, expert fees, or barristers. Many barristers, often the good ones, will not do no win no fee and so you need to budget for these additional expenses. Although in practice no win no fee means that you have to part with a percentage of your winnings, the wording of the retainer allows the solicitor to charge a "success fee" which can increase his hourly rate up to 100%. You are then liable for this uplifted part of his hourly rate upon winning. What he does though is cap this uplift at 25% of your winnings so they do not all get gobbled up by this uplift. While the other side are liable for nearly all other costs if they lose (except after the event insurance) they are not liable for the success fee uplift.

Contingency Agreement: Any arrangement with your solicitor where their fees are only paid contingent upon a successful outcome.

Damages-Based Agreement: Another form of contingency arrangement like no win no fee, but more purely taking a percentage of your winnings and nothing else. Only common in very high value cases and sometimes for small claims at the higher end. Because they are a new invention and not really working properly at the current time, you will be lucky to find a solicitor who will do one.

Default Judgment: This usually applies where your opponent ignores your claim. You are unlikely to get it if all they have done is miss a court deadline by a few days. Note that it can often be set aside, sometimes quite easily. If your opponent does this, make sure to hit them with the costs of wasting your time and court time. For instance, you may have to apply to the court using an N244 form for default judgment, which incurs a court fee.

Directions Questionnaire: This is a very important document because it basically lays out the rules of engagement, for instance what track your claim will be on, how long the trial is likely to last, how many witnesses you need and whether you need an expert. You are settling up the parameters of the dogfight so take care with this form and always try and be professional and liaise with the other side.

Disclosure: Civil litigation is split into phases, and the disclosure phase is the key point at which you have to disclose your evidence to the other side. It only happens after the statements have all been filed and served and a court usually will send out an order laying out the disclosure process, although it is also explained in the CPR. The purpose of disclosure is to collect the evidence that you will then use to exhibit as documents to your witness statement, the next phase after disclosure. You can also make an application for disclosure very early, before proceedings are issued, but only do this if there really is critical evidence without which it is impossible to get your claim off the ground. (And you can actually point to this evidence. The courts do not like "fishing expeditions".)

Detailed Assessment: Costs Proceedings, made by means of the Part 8 procedure.

Early Neutral Evaluation: A new type of alternative dispute resolution, that involves an opinion on the strengths of the case, so that parties can more easily come to settlement. It is like a mini or provisional judgment based on what evidence there is at the time. Mediators usually refrain from expressing a view on the merits of a case, which is why it could be a useful alternative to mediation and may grow in popularity in the future as courts come increasingly under strain.

Enforcement: The procedure you follow after you have judgment and want to get your money!

Exhibits: The documents that are the critical evidence that you "exhibit" with your witness statement.

Fast-Track: Claims between £10,000 - £25,000 are usually allocated to the fast track, but be aware it is not automatic and some complex claims or claims with lots of witnesses may be allocated to the multi-track (or conversely allocated down to small claims). For trials of one day.

Fee Remission: You may not have to pay court fees if you are on benefits.

File: Send to court.

Legal Surgery: Something law firms are increasingly pioneering as a low-cost way to get access to a lawyer who will read documents during that hour and is far more feasible by the change to the online world. A necessity these days as legal aid dries up and more and more people have to pay for legal advice.

Letter of Claim: The critical letter that clearly lays out your claim and is an essential precursor to issuing proceedings.

Limitations: Causes of action have time-frames after which you can no longer bring a claim. So typically for personal injury it is 3 years and negligence or contract is 6 years. If you bring a claim out of time it is not necessarily fatal, but a defendant will certainly make a major issue of it in their defence. But the time-frames are not set in stone or absolute.

Litigant in person: Someone who represents themselves in their own case.

McKenzie Friend: Someone who helps a litigant in person run their case, but only in exceptional circumstances will the court allow them to actually do all the work, such as presenting the case in court. They are meant to assist, not take charge.

Mediation: A popular type of alternative dispute resolution that courts are hot on these days. On the small claims track you will be offered mediation and you should probably accept it. In other areas you can do it before proceedings, or you can ask for a stay and do it after proceedings have been issued. It usually takes a day, in the average-sized claim, and can be expensive as you need to pay for a mediator, three rooms, and perhaps your own lawyer if you are using one. In the future of course people may do them online, which will obviously save costs.

Multi-Track: County court claims of a value over £25,000. But remember this is not the only criteria. The trial will be two days or more.

No Win No Fee: See conditional fee agreement. Same thing.

Part 7: Most money claims are made using the Part 7 procedure and are usually basic money claims. Part 8 is for special cases.

Part 36 Offers: Special types of offers which have specific rules if a party fails to beat that offer at trial, leading to the person who has failed to beat an offer (win or lose) taking a big hit on costs. I do not encourage litigants in person to try to master them, but perhaps take some tailored legal advice. This is because they can also use a normal without prejudice offer and a court will also give you benefit for this, though not as much as for Part 36. Do not use them in small claims.

Part 18 Request: A formal way of getting your opponent to ask specific questions, key to your case. This forms part of the pleadings or statements of case and so the judge will be careful to focus on it, more than he would on a simple letter, for instance.

Pleadings: See statements of case.

Practice Directions: To be found alongside the CPR, guidance to help you with the rules and how to follow them properly.

Pre-Action Disclosure: See disclosure, above.

Pre-Action Protocols: The codes enshrined in the CPR which tell you what you have to do pre-issue and the hoops you have to jump through. So do not just shoot from the hip and issue proceedings without having followed the protocols. For most claims the General Pre-action Protocol will apply. (Personal injury claims, larger building disputes and other claims like defamation, for instance, have their own specific protocols.)

Precedent H: See budgets, above. The complex spreadsheet that has to be used in multi-track claims where parties are represented.

Reply: A document that forms part of the statements of case, or pleadings, and is used by a claimant to respond to a defence, or a defendant to respond to a defence to a counterclaim. Not essential, but sometimes helpful in clarifying things you may have missed in your defence or particulars of claim.

Retainers: The fancy word for the contract between you and your solicitor.

Serve: Send to your opponent.

Settlement Agreement: Nearly all cases never go to trial and instead a settlement agreement is drafted, often with a Tomlin order, to bring proceedings to an end.

Small Claims Track: Claims of a value lower than £10,000 and a half-day in length but remember this is not the only criteria, just the main starting point. Trials of half a day. The track where special rules means lawyers are usually (although not always) kept out, because only in exceptional circumstances will you get your legal costs back from the other side if you win.

Statements of Case: Same thing as pleadings. Lays out the factual basis of your case and the basic story and focuses on the relevant issues and is designed to tease these relevant issues out. It is not to be used to give evidence, which is the domain of witness statements. The shorter and more concise the better and the CPR actually requires they be concise.

Strike-Out Application: A powerful weapon that is often used by bigger, well-funded opponents like banks, public bodies and corporations, who will use it to expose weaknesses in your drafted case, even though your case may be at heart a strong one. Bring a claim poorly on the papers and you could face a whopping bill before the plane is even off the ground, as they are often made early on, sometimes even before your opponent has filed a defence. If you lose the hearing you end up having to pay your opponent's costs of that hearing. This acts as a powerful dis-incentive to the faint-hearted to continue with a poorly-drafted claim.

Substantive law: The underlying main law, rather than procedural law.

Summary Judgment: If you think your opponent's case is so weak as to not reach a basic threshold then you can make this early on, often tactically. But be careful, as a judge may be very reluctant to make an early decision without having seen the full evidence, unless of course the opponent looks to be just trying it on, buying time, or is a vexatious litigant.

Trial Bundles: As it says, the bundled set of documents that usually the claimant must produce in advance of the trial and send around to everyone. The court will usually order the timing of this. Allow yourself time as it is more time-consuming than you think and always ensure you liaise with your opponent about what goes in so you do not turn up at court with a bundle your opponent does not agree with. One of those points in the litigation cycle where you need to be professional and co-operate with your opponent.

The White Book: Only barristers should use this hefty legal tome with case authorities on how to interpret the CPR. You can easily go down the rabbit hole with the White Book if you are not a barrister and so better to just focus on the CPR and the plain and common-sense reasoning of the rules and practice directions.

Tomlin Order: The document that is usually required in conjunction with a settlement agreement to formally bring proceedings to an end.

Without Prejudice: What you write on an offer letter which then will not be disclosed until after the judge has made his decision and is considering what costs award he should make. A Part 36 offer is a without prejudice offer.

Without Prejudice Save as To Costs: An offer that is designed to be able to be disclosed in costs proceedings (but not before), should they be necessary on the fast or multi-track.

Witness Statement: Exchanged at a specific date and simultaneously. The document which exhibits your evidence, as opposed to your pleadings or statement of case (which lays out the facts as you say they happened and focuses on the issues). The witness statement is to provide the evidence to prove what you say in your statement of case is right. Do not confuse the two.

ABOUT THE AUTHOR

Alex Woods is a solicitor and litigation specialist with over 25 years of experience in the courts of England and Wales. Since he runs a law firm, he deals daily with all sorts of general litigation, whether representing clients in the courts himself or giving people advice and assistance over the phone when they run their case themselves, just as you may be about to.

Cases that he has worked on include building disputes (acting for both business and individuals), negligence disputes between neighbours, professional negligence (accountants and solicitors), financial mis-selling litigation (suing banks), contractual disputes, landlord and tenant, personal injury, small-scale commercial disputes, cohabitation property disputes, contested will disputes and inheritance act claims. One new area in which Redwood Legal now provides access to justice is representing foreign businesses against UK-based opponents who are trying to use cross-border issues to evade debts.

He passionately believes in access to justice, ever since he came up against the problem of large, rich businesses and corporations who intimidate opponents with the cost of legal proceedings. He first came across this as a young lawyer whilst working for his father's small business in Colchester, Essex, involving a dispute with a well-known construction company. This is why the law firm now specialises in "no win no fee" cases, provides discounted and fixed-fee services for litigants in person, and why it runs a YouTube channel providing people with advice and assistance on running their claims. More recently, it created the CourtWingman (dot) com website.

Sometimes clients do not need full representation and just rely on the free materials or and the odd phone call. Alex Woods likes nothing more than when people are able to run their claims with minimal help. One recent example is a follower who had been faithfully following the free materials on YouTube and had written a long thank-you note, attaching the actual copy of the judgment that had been made in his favour! He had won without paying a penny to lawyers.

Before establishing the law firm, Alex Woods was passionate about financial mis-selling and represented many clients against the banks at the time of the 2008 recession (payment protection insurance and interest rate swaps). He appeared on BBC's popular daytime television show with Angela Rippon, Julia Somerville and Gloria Hunniford, "Rip Off Britain!".

Made in United States
North Haven, CT
14 March 2024